APRIL SHOWERS

Leslie M Farrell

BookLeaf
Publishing

India | USA | UK

April Showers © 2021 Leslie M Farrell

Presentation by *BookLeaf Publishing*

Web: www.bookleafpub.com

E-mail: info@bookleafpub.com

ISBN: 9789358738599

First edition 2021

ACKNOWLEDGEMENTS

I would like to thank myself for writing this book. More people should thank themselves; it feels great!

PREFACE

The collection you are about to read was written in a month.

Now, when you inevitably flip forward and notice how short this collection is, you might think that this is not a big deal, but let me explain:

Poetry is hard.

I have never considered myself a poet, at least, not a good one. I love poetry and hold it up as one of the highest forms of art, so to consider myself as belonging to that elite class of beings who are able to create such art was unthinkable.

Still, I wrote poetry. I mean what depressed and angsty teen hasn't? Was it good? No. Did it feel good? Yes. And really, isn't that one of the things poetry does best: help to release the demons inside of us, or alleviate the ecstasy that is threatening to burst, or allow us to explain just how much we love that Grecian urn? Poetry was a nonjudgmental and welcoming friend who supported all of the odd and nonsensical half-thoughts that my mixed-up feelings were spilling forth.

And this was enough for me. I was content to keep them as scribbles in the margins of my notebooks, or scattered on random post-it notes around the house.

That is until I came across an advertisement from a little publishing company on a lazy afternoon. For a small fee, they said, you could have your very own book of poetry, all you had to do was write one poem every day for a month.

And like the nonrealistic dreamer I am, I thought, "Sounds doable!"

After all, I was in-between projects, and had a handful of poems from the recesses of my youth, how hard could coming up with thirty poems actually be?

Wrong, wrong, wrong!

It turns out that thirty is a big number when you think about it. In vain I scanned my documents for usable material, quickly discovering that, like with most things in my life, I was a genius in my own mind, but not so much on paper.

But I had paid the fee, and the first day of the challenge was already upon me, so I would have to plow on.

Thankfully, I was saved. Saved by one special poem that would ignite the spark that would become April Showers. A poem about a darkness that enters a town. It got me to thinking: What had happened to that town after the darkness had come in? What had the townspeople done within it? And, more importantly, did they let it stay? This was the story that I wanted to tell.

This poem, this shining beacon of light, would be THE BEGINNING and would allow me to do what I do best, put way too much thought into way too few words.

I wrote this collection in a month, but really, it is the result of a lifetime of work. Of countless bad poems written, of endless hours submerged in my own darkness, and of innumerable days spent in sunshine with the people that I love. It has all brought me to this point where I could dig and scrounge and sweat and toil to produce the work currently in your hands.

This collection may seem like it is full of darkness, but really, there is love behind every word.

P.S. In case you were wondering, writing a preface is also very difficult.

This book is dedicated to all of those who are suffering from depression, anxiety, or any other form of mental illness. I would like to say that it gets better, but really, you just get better at getting better, which, for me at least, has turned out to be better than better anyway.

1. THE BEGINNING

The big black storm clouds appeared suddenly

at the edge of town.

Full of electricity.

Charged with centuries of fear and hate, so palpable

it made our hair stand on end as we stood in the square,

staring, unblinking, at the mass

of swirling and eddying

vapor.

It sat as a wall against the houseline,

longing to invade,

to cover the places where we lived and laughed,

eager to seep into the cracks of our foundation, creating

ribbons of destruction and rivers of violence.

But it did not breach.

This monstrosity,

stilted against an invisible barrier,

held back by our lack of

invitation,

wanted and watched

for a tipping point.

For a breezy invitation that would let it in. Let it corrupt.

And we decided, best to leave it alone.

But the waiting became too much,

the looming darkness became too heavy,

and the watching, waiting people became too restless.

So we opened our arms,

and let it in.

We watched with gratitude as it covered the harsh sun.

We breathed it in with jittery anticipation,

letting it cloud our minds;

and rest deep inside our souls.

2. THE CLOUD

Darkest Depths where the pain resides

Crawling and Creeping, infecting my insides

Consuming me from the inside out

Leaving me in confusion and Doubt

The light is gone where I know stand

I walk in shadows, in the land of the Dead

The screaming and chortling is music to my ears

I Love the Sound of loved ones calling out to their Dears

"Oh save me, Save me!" they pathetically Cry

But I take their Life and Toss it aside

The Fires that consume my every thought

Are unleashed in the mind in hideous plots

Plots of Murder, Plots of Sin

Plots that take life from Within

No one can save you from my hideous face

I bestow on all a Dark and Deceiving grace

Grace of Wealth, Grace of Glory

Grace of Madness Grace of Fury!

All succumb to my evil stare

There are none to defeat me, none dare!

I am the victor in this game of Death

Who may stop me, who has the breath?

The answer is no one, there is none

Not even the rising and setting Sun!

I am all Power and Wrath and Greediness galore!

Just wait till you see what I have in store

For your children will want to have me on their side

And your children's children will want me as their guide

I am everlasting, I will not fade

Throughout the ages I will not be tamed

I will take without mercy the innocent and helpless

I care not what side support this

This infestation of Greed and Want

Which only ends when I begin to taunt

You asked me to come and so here I am

Succumb to my Power, and become one of the damned.

3. THE HOUSE DOWN THE STREET

The faucet in the back right corner

of the back left bathroom

of the top top floor,

would

not

stop

dripping.

4. THE FARMHOUSE

The window next to the silken wall

was crawling with

dirt.

5. THE OTHER SIDE OF TOWN

The floorboards creaked

beneath her pounding head

as he came

home

from the bar.

6. THE SCHOOL

The ink meant for the

page

was seeping into the brand new

desks.

7. THE SHOP

The rusted old scissors were laying unused

next to the miles of unedited fabric.

8. THE JAIL

The hard wooden chair

sat so lonely,

its halo of electricity calling out to

provide.

9. THE MAYOR'S OFFICE

The nice wooden desk in

the center of the room,

was eaten away by

mold.

10. THE BARSTOOL

The sticky, stale, sweet, scent

was poisoning my nostrils.

11. THE CENTER OF TOWN

The courthouse stood,

completely still.

12. THE TRAFFIC LIGHT

The light shone red upon

the one solitary car in the lane.

13. THE LIBRARY

The rising water from the basement

was coming up to greet the

sinking shelves.

14. THE HOLE

The empty pit in my chest was weighing me down

into the sheets,

making my eyelids heavy,

and my soul weak.

15. THE ECKSTEIN'S

The noisy tea kettle's steam

overwhelmed the one-room cabin,

completely blocking out

the wood-burning stove.

16. AT THE ECKSTEIN'S

She turned on the lamp

too late,

for he had already

taken out the knife.

17. OUT OF THE HOLE

The hole in my chest lightens just enough,

to see the bottle of pills

on my bedside table.

18. FROM THE LIBRARY

The rising water from the basement

greets

the sinking shelves,

the twisted metal taking her by the hair

to embrace the

icy waters.

19. AT THE TRAFFIC LIGHT

The light shines red upon

the one crumpled solitary car

wrapped around its delicate base.

20. IN THE CENTER OF TOWN

The courthouse stands completely still.

21. ON THE BARSTOOL

The sticky, stale, sweet, scent

poisons my sight

as he sputters next to me,

his face the color of

the walls.

22. IN THE MAYOR'S OFFICE

The nice wooden desk in

the center of the room

warms the eyes with its

delicate flames.

23. FROM THE JAIL

The hard wooden chair

no longer sits lonely,

its halo of electricity illuminating

the skeleton

inside.

24. AT THE SHOP

The rusted old scissors lay

next to the miles of unedited fabric,

drenched in a scarlet red

gleam.

25. IN THE SCHOOL

A little swinging shadow

hovers over the

ink-stained desks.

26. ON THE OTHER SIDE OF TOWN

The floorboards creak

as his body hits the

floor.

27. AT THE FARMHOUSE

The window gets

cleaned with

broken fingers.

28. DOWN THE STREET

The blood from her wrist

Will

Not

Stop

Dripping…

29. THE CHANCE

Maybe the half-eaten rosebush

in the back corner of

our yard,

does not have to be our own.

30. CONCLUSION

We stare at our once perfectly white walls.

They are forever marred in crimson hate,

in a messy mosaic of haste,

rotting into the bones of our houses.

Are we able to live with it?

Already the cloud above us is dissipating,

harsh sunlight leaking through to highlight our sins,

the heat burning them deeper into the drywall.

It is too much.

We pick up our paintbrushes,

laden in a black, inky mask,

and go over it all, covering every last drop.

Choosing to live in the dark.

843508LV00012B/2513